EASY LETTER NOTES

CLASSICAL PIECES

61 songs

playinoneday.com

Book design 1st edition Krakow 2021
Play In One Day - playinoneday.com
Publisher

contact@playinoneday.com
Contact email

Contents

Contents

Contents

EASY LETTER NOTES

CLASSICAL PIECES

61 songs

Basics of learning to play the piano

Sound names:

Each key on the keyboard (or any other keyboard instrument) corresponds to one of the letters: C, D, E, F, G, A, B. You can best understand this by looking at the picture below.

Some of the white keys have shorter black keys in between.

- The black key to the right of the C key is the C# key.
- The black key to the right of the D key is the D# key.
- There is no black key to the right of the E key.
- The black key to the right of the F key is the F# key.
- The black key to the right of the G key is the G# key.
- The black key to the right of the A key is the A# key.
- There is no black key to the right of the B key.

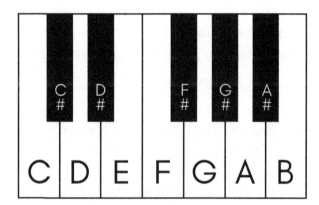

Description of the entire keyboard:

The above pattern (C, D, E, F, G, A, B) is repeated several times on your instrument's keyboard. So that the letters do not get confused, we add numbers to them depending on their position on the keyboard.

- **In the very centre** of the keyboard, the letters have no numbers added.
- They are numbered **2 to the right** of the keyboard, and 3 further to the right.
- They are numbered **-2 to the left** of the keyboard, and -3 further to the left.

As in the drawing:

Learning to play in three steps

STEP 1 - Practice the key names and play with your right hand.

If you are just starting to learn to play the piano, a good way to remember all the names of the keys (C, D, E, F, G, A, B) is to only learn to play with your right hand.

Just ignore the left hand notes (the ones in the squares) and play only with your right hand. Thanks to this, you will practice the names of the keys well and get used to the keyboard.

You will switch to the two-handed game once you have mastered the names of all the keys.

Always listen to the recordings (page 15) before learning to play!

STEP 2 - Combine right and left hand play.

You already know keys names and can play with your right hand? Add your left hand.

Now if you see a square with a letter in the middle above the note for your right hand - press this key with your left hand.

Continue the game with your right hand and keep the key pressed with your left hand until you come across the next square with the letter in the middle.

Note,
some songs may not sound right when playing the left hand with just one key. You will be able to play them when you go to step 3.

STEP 3 - A two-handed game with chords.

Two-handed play is no longer a problem for you?
Instead of playing only single notes with your left hand, play whole chords
(3 keys at the same time).

If, for example, you see the letter "C" in a square, then instead of playing only the C note with your left hand, play the entire C chord.

You will find a list of all the chords and keys you need to press to play them in the attached chord table (page 13).

It is best to practice all the chords in the song first before playing it.

Frequently asked questions

1. What do our letter notes look like:

Our letter notes allow you to play with two hands. **Larger letters represent the notes for the right hand. Smaller letters in the squares represent the notes (chords) for the left hand.**

Play with the left hand

Play with the right hand

Are you sleeping?

2. Where to play the chords:

If you're wondering where to play the chords, look at the figure below:

play chords here
(left hand)

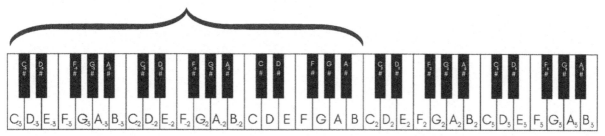

In fact, you can also play the chords where you think they sound good. It's not rigidly defined.

3. There is only a verse and a chorus in the notes, how do you play the whole song?

In the notes, you will most often find a verse and a chorus. The songs are arranged as follows:

Verse - chorus - verse - chorus - verse - chorus etc.

Therefore, to play the whole thing - just repeat the verse and chorus (each verse and each chorus is played to the same melody).

Sometimes there is only a chorus in the notes. This means the song has no verse and the layout is:

chorus - chorus - chorus etc.

playinoneday.com

That's all you need to know to play the letter notes.

MAJOR CHORDS

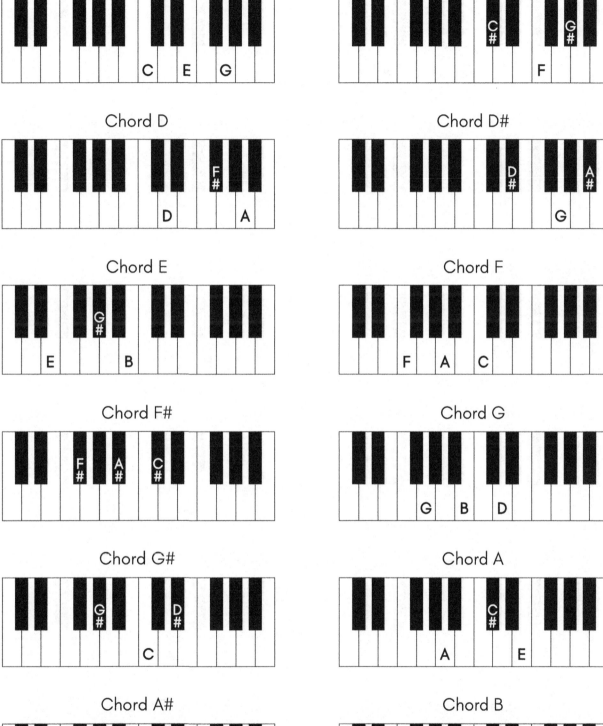

Chord C

Chord C#

Chord D

Chord D#

Chord E

Chord F

Chord F#

Chord G

Chord G#

Chord A

Chord A#

Chord B

MINOR CHORDS

Chord c

Chord c#

Chord d

Chord d#

Chord e

Chord f

Chord f#

Chord g

Chord g#

Chord a

Chord a#

Chord b

Recording to all of the songs can be found there:

www.playinoneday.com/recordings

SCAN ME!

Stickers for your piano

C_{-3} D_{-3} E_{-3} F_{-3} G_{-3} A_{-3} B_{-3}

C_{-2} D_{-2} E_{-2} F_{-2} G_{-2} A_{-2} B_{-2}

C D E F G A B

C_2 D_2 E_2 F_2 G_2 A_2 B_2

C_3 D_3 E_3 F_3 G_3 A_3 B_3

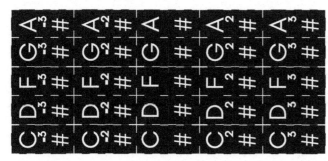

How to set up stickers

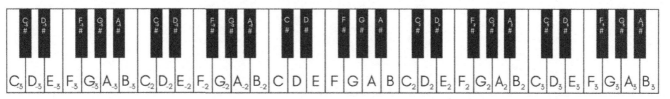

"If your instrument has more keys than in the diagram, sticker with C (without number) should be in the center of your keyboard (The extra keys on the sides of the instrument will not be covered)

Stickers for your piano

Pick a song and start playing!

20th Century Fox Fanfare

[C] G_2 G_2 G_2 G_2 $G\#_2$

G_2 $G\#_2$ G_2 $G\#_2$

[C] G_2 G_2 G_2 G_2 G_2 G_2 G_2

G_2 G_2 G_2 E_2 F_2

[C] G_2 G_2 G_2 C_2 E_2 G_2 [F] A_2 D_2 F_2 A_2

[d] C_3 D_2 F_2 $G\#_2$ [C] C_3 G_2 E_2 F_2 G_2

Alla turca

B A G# A [a]C_2 D_2 C_2 B C_2

[a]E_2 F_2 E_2 $D\#_2$ E_2 [a]B_2 A_2

$G\#_2$ A_2 B_2 $G\#_2$ A_2

[a]C_3 A_2 C_3 [e]B_2 A_2 G_2 A_2

B_2 A_2 G_2 A_2 [e]B_2 A_2 [B]G_2 $F\#_2$

[e]E_2 B A G# A [a]C_2 D_2 C_2 B C_2

[a]E_2 F_2 E_2 $D\#_2$ E_2 [a]B_2 A_2

$G\#_2$ A_2 B_2 A_2 $G\#_2$ A_2

[a]C_3 A_2 C_3 [e]B_2 A_2 G_2 A_2

B_2 A_2 G_2 A_2 [e]B_2 A_2 G_2 A_2

B_2 A_2 G_2 A_2 [e]B_2 A_2 [B]G_2 $F\#_2$

[e]E_2 E_2 F_2 [C]G_2 G A_2 G_2 F_2 E_2

[G] D_2 E_2 F_2 [C] G_2 G_2 A_2 G_2 F_2 E_2

[G] D_2 C_2 D_2 [a] E_2 E_2 F_2 E_2 D_2 C_2

[E] B C_2 D_2 [a] E_2 E_2 F_2 E_2 D_2 C_2

[E] B B A G# A [a] C_2 D_2 C_2 B C_2

[a] E_2 F_2 E_2 $D\#_2$ E_2 [a] B_2 A_2

$G\#_2$ A_2 B_2 A_2 $G\#_2$ A_2

[D#] C_3 A_2 B_2 [a] C_3 B_2 [d] A_2 $G\#_2$

[a] A_2 E_2 F_2 [d] D_2 [E] C_2 B

[a] A A B [A] $C\#_2$ A B

[A] $C\#_2$ B A G# [D] F# G# [B] A B

[E] G# E A B [A] $C\#_2$ A B

[A] $C\#_2$ B A G# [D] F# B [E] G# E

[A] A A B [A] $C\#_2$ A B

[A] C#$_2$ B A G# [D] F# G# [B] A B

[E] G# E A B [A] C#$_2$ A B

[A] C#$_2$ B A G# [D] F# B [E] G# E [A] A

Can can

[G] G D$_2$ D$_2$ E$_2$ [C] D$_2$ C$_2$ C$_2$ E$_2$

[F] F$_2$ A$_2$ [C] A$_2$ G$_2$ G$_2$

[G] A$_2$ B B A$_2$ [C] G$_2$ C$_2$ C$_2$ E$_2$

[D] E$_2$ D$_2$ E$_2$ D$_2$ [G] E$_2$ D$_2$ E$_2$ D$_2$

[G] G D$_2$ D$_2$ E$_2$ [C] D$_2$ C$_2$ C$_2$ E$_2$

[F] F$_2$ A$_2$ C$_3$ A$_2$ [C] A$_2$ G$_2$ G$_2$

[G] A$_2$ B B A$_2$ [C] G$_2$ C$_2$ C$_2$ E$_2$

[G] E$_2$ D$_2$ E$_2$ D$_2$ [C] D$_2$ C$_2$ C$_2$

[C] E$_2$ C$_2$ A G [G] G$_2$ D$_2$ E$_2$ F$_2$ [C] E$_2$ D$_2$ C$_2$

[C] E$_2$ C$_2$ A G F# G A B [G] D$_2$ C$_2$ C$_2$

[C] E$_2$ C$_2$ A G [G] G$_2$ D$_2$ E$_2$ F$_2$ [C] E$_2$ D$_2$ C$_2$

[C] E$_2$ C$_2$ A G F# G A B [C] C$_2$ G [G] B G

$\boxed{C}$ $\boxed{G}$ $\boxed{C}$ $\boxed{G}$ $\boxed{C}$
C_2 G B C_2 G B G C_2 G

$\boxed{G}$ $\boxed{C}$
B G C_2 C_2 C_2 C_2

$\boxed{C}$ $\boxed{C}$
C_2 C_2 C_2 C_2 C_2 C_2 C_2 C_2

$\boxed{C}$ $\boxed{F}$
C_2 C_2 C_2 C_2 F

Colonel Bogey March

[C] C₂ B A [C] G E C E [G] G G A G G A [G] G

[C] G E [C] E F G [C] E₂ E₂ C₂ [C] G E

[C] E F E G G F [d] F [G] D

[G] D E F [C] G E

[a] E F# E [G] D G E

[D] F# D A [G] G [C] G E

[C] E F G [C] E₂ E₂ C₂ [C] G E

[C] E F E G [d] G F

[G] F D [G] A B A [C] C₂ G [a] G F E

[d] D A C B₋₂ [G] G B₋₂ [C] C E E

[a] C₂ B A [a] G# A G F E F E

[a] A [E] G# A [a] C₂ A [A] D#₂ D#₂

E₂ D₂ C₂ B A G# A D F E D

C B₋₂ A₋₂ E B₋₂ C A₋₂

G E E F G E₂ E₂ C₂

G E E F E G G F

F D D E F G E

E F# E D G E F# D A G

G E E F G E₂ E₂ C₂

G E E F E

G G F F D A B A C₂ G

G F E D A C B₋₂ G B₋₂ C

Dance of the Knights

[a] E A C$_2$ E$_2$ A$_2$ E$_2$ C$_2$ A

[a] E A C$_2$ E$_2$ A$_2$ E$_2$

G$_2$ B$_2$ E$_3$ G$_3$ E$_3$ B$_2$ G$_2$

[e] E$_2$ G$_2$ B$_2$ E$_3$ G$_3$

G#$_3$ G$_3$ F#$_3$ [c] G$_2$ G$_3$ [G] G$_2$ G#$_2$ G$_2$ F#$_2$ F#$_2$ F#$_2$ [c] G$_2$ G

G# G F# G# G F# C$_2$ B [E] E

A C$_2$ E$_2$ A$_2$ E$_2$ C$_2$ A

[a] E A C$_2$ E$_2$ A$_2$ E$_2$

G$_2$ B$_2$ E$_3$ G$_3$ E$_3$ B$_2$ G$_2$

[e] E$_2$ G$_2$ B$_2$ B$_2$

C$_3$ B$_2$ A#$_2$ A#$_2$ A#$_2$ [e] A#$_2$ B

[B] A# C$_2$ B D#$_3$ [e] A#$_2$ B

29

[F] B   D#$_2$ G#$_2$ B$_2$ [g#] D#$_3$ G#$_3$ B$_2$

D#$_3$ [F] D#$_3$ [E] G#$_3$ G#$_3$ G#$_3$ [a] A$_3$

For Elise

E_2 D#$_2$ E_2 D#$_2$ E_2 B D_2 C_2

[a] A C E A [E] B E G# B

[a] C_2 E E_2 D#$_2$ E_2 D#$_2$ E_2 B D_2 C_2

[a] A C E A [E] B E C_2 B

[a] A B [G] C_2 D_2 [C] E_2 G F_2 E_2

[G] D_2 F E_2 D_2 [a] C_2 E D_2 C_2

[E] B E E_2 D#$_2$ E_2 D#$_2$

E_2 D#$_2$ E_2 B D_2 C_2 [a] A C E A

[E] B E G# B [a] C_2 E E_2 D#$_2$

E_2 D#$_2$ E_2 B D_2 C_2 [a] A C E A

[E] B E C_2 B [a] A

Eine Kleine Nachtmusik

[C] C_3 G_2 C_3 G_2 [C] C_3 G_2 C_3 E_3 G_3

[G] F_3 D F D [G] F_3 D_3 B_2 D_3 G_2

[C] C_3 C_3 E_3 D_3 C_3 [G] C_3 B_2 B_2 D_3 F_3 B_2

[C] D_3 C_3 C_3 E_3 D_3 C_3 [G] C_3 B_2 B_2 D_3 F_3 B_2

[C] C_3 C_3 C_3 B_2 A_2 B_2 [C] C_3 C_3 E_3 D_3 C_3 D_3

[C] E_3 E_3 G_3 F_3 E_3 F_3 G_3

[C] G_2 [F] A_2 [G] G_2 F_2 F_2 [C] F_2 E_2 E_2

[d] E_2 D_2 D_2 [G] C_2 B A B [C] C_2 [G]

Entry of the gladiators

[C] E E E E E E [C]

[D] F# F# F# F# F# F# [D] F#

[G] G G G G G G [G]

[C] C₂ B A# B A# A G# G F# G

[C] A G# G G# G F# F E D# E

[G] G D D C# D G D D C# D

[G] B₋₂ C C# D D# E F F# G G# A B A G

[C] C₂ B A# B A# A G# G F# G

[C] A G# G G# G F# F E D# E

[B] D# D# D# F# B₋₂ [e] G A G F# E B₋₂

[B] B B B B B B B B B

33

Hallelujah from ,,The Messiah"

[C] C G A G [C] C₂ E F E

G [G] F E D [C] C G₋₂ A₋₂ B₋₂

[C] C₂ G A G

[C] C₂ G A G G G [C] A G

G G A G C₂ [G] B C₂ B [C] C₂

[G] D₂ G E₂ D₂ [G] D₂ G E₂ D₂

D₂ D₂ [G] E₂ D₂ D₂ D₂ E₂ D₂ D₂

[D] E₂ D₂ C₂ [G] B

In the hall of the Mountain King

[a] A_{-2} B_{-2} C D [a] E C E

[B] D# B_{-2} D# [A#] D $A\#_{-2}$ D

[a] A_{-2} B_{-2} C D [a] E C E A

[C] G E C E G

[a] A_{-2} B_{-2} C D [a] E C E

[B] D# B_{-2} D# [A#] D $A\#_{-2}$ D

[a] A_{-2} B_{-2} C D [a] E C E A

[C] G E C E G

[E] E F# G# A B G# B

[C] C_2 G# C_2 [E] B G# B

[E] E F# G# A B G# B

[C] C_2 G# $C\#_2$ [E] B

[E] E F# G# A B G# B

[c#] C#₂ G# C#₂ [E] B G# B

[E] E F# G# A B G# B

[c#] C#₂ G# C#₂ [E] B

Jarabe tapatio

[G] G₂ G₂ F#₂ [C] G₂ E₂ D#₂ E₂ C₂ B C₂ G

E F [C] G A B C₂ D₂ E₂ [G] F₂ D₂

F₂ E₂ [G] F₂ D₂ C#₂ D₂ B A# B G

G₂ G₂ [G] G₂ A₂ G₂ F₂ E₂ D₂ [C] C₂

G₂ F#₂ [C] G₂ E₂ D#₂ E₂ C₂ B C₂ G

E F [C] G A B C₂ D₂ E₂ [G] F₂ D₂

F₂ E₂ [G] F₂ D₂ C#₂ D₂ B A# B G

G₂ G₂ [G] G₂ A₂ G₂ F₂ E₂ D₂ [C] C₂

La raspa

G [C] C$_2$ G C$_2$ G C$_2$

G [C] C$_2$ D$_2$ C$_2$ B C$_2$ [G] D$_2$

G [G] B G B G B

G [G] B C$_2$ B A B [C] C$_2$

G [C] C$_2$ G C$_2$ G C$_2$

G [C] C$_2$ D$_2$ C$_2$ B C$_2$ [G] D$_2$

G [G] B G B G B

G [G] B C$_2$ B A B [C] C$_2$

La donna e mobile (Rigoletto, Verdi)

[C] E_2 E_2 E_2 [G] G_2 F_2 D_2

[G] D_2 D_2 D_2 [C] F_2 E_2 C_2

[C] E_2 D_2 C_2 [G] C_2 B

[G] D_2 C_2 A [C] A G

[C] E_2 E_2 E_2 [G] G_2 F_2 D_2

[G] D_2 D_2 D_2 [C] F_2 E_2 C_2

[C] E_2 D_2 C_2 [G] C_2 B

[G] D_2 C_2 A [C] A G

Wedding March

C C C C C C C C C C C

E E E E E E E E G G G G G G G

[C] [B] [e] [F]
C₂ B F# A G F D

[C] [G] [C]
C D G₋₂ D E G₋₂ C E C E G

[C] [B] [e] [F]
C₂ B F# A G F D

[C] [G] [C] [C]
C E D E D C C₂

[B] [e] [F]
B F# A G F D

[C] [G] [C]
C D G₋₂ D E G₋₂ C E C E G

[C] [B] [e] [F]
C₂ B F# A G F D

[C] [G] [C]
C E D E D C C

[G]
C C₂ C₂ E₂ D₂ B G

[C] [G]
G C₂ C₂ E₂ E₂ D₂ B G

40

G E$_2$ E$_2$ G$_2$ G$_2$ F$_2$ E$_2$

D$_2$ C#$_2$ E$_2$ D$_2$ A C$_2$ B G A B

C$_2$ B F# A G F D

C D G$_{-2}$ D

E G$_{-2}$ C E C E G C$_2$

B F# A G F D

C E D E D C

Funeral March

[a] [F] [a] [F]
A_{-2} A_{-2} A_{-2} A_{-2} C B_{-2}

[a] [F] [a] [F]
B_{-2} A_{-2} A_{-2} A_{-2} A_{-2}

[a] [F] [a] [F] [a] [F] [a] [F]
C C C C E D D C C C C

[a] [F] [a] [F] [a] [F] [a] [F]
A G F E E C A G F E E C

[a] [F] [a] [F] [a] [F] [a] [F]
A_{-2} A_{-2} A_{-2} A_{-2} C B_{-2} B_{-2} A_{-2} A_{-2} A_{-2} B_{-2}

[a] [F] [a] [F] [a] [F] [a] [F]
A_{2} G_{2} F_{2} E_{2} E_{2} C_{2} A_{2} G_{2} F_{2} E_{2} E_{2} C_{2}

[a] [F] [a] [F] [a] [F] [a] [G]
A A A A C_{2} B B A A A A B

[C] [C] [C] [G]
C_{2} E_{2} F_{2} G_{2} A_{2} B_{2} C_{3} E_{3} D_{3} F_{2}

[a] [a] [B] [E]
E_{2} E_{2} $F\#_{2}$ $G\#_{2}$ A_{2} B_{2} C_{3} C B_{2}

[G] [C] [E] [F]
G_{2} C_{3} E_{2} F_{2} E_{2} C_{2}

[a] [F] [a] [F] [a] [F] [a]
A A A A C_{2} B B A A A A

Minuet in G

[C] G_2 C_2 D_2 E_2 F_2 [C] G_2 C_2 C_2

[F] A_2 F_2 G_2 A_2 B_2 [C] C_3 C_2 C_2

[F] F_2 G_2 F_2 E_2 D_2 [C] E_2 F_2 E_2 D_2 C_2

[G] B C_2 D_2 E_2 C_2 [G] D_2

[C] G_2 C_2 D_2 E_2 F_2 [C] G_2 C_2 C_2

[F] A_2 F_2 G_2 A_2 B_2 [C] C_3 C_2 C_2

[F] F_2 G_2 F_2 E_2 D_2 [C] E_2 F_2 E_2 D_2 C_2

[G] D_2 E_2 D_2 C_2 B [C] C_2

Nocturne op.9 no.2

G [C]E_2 D_2 E_2 [C]D_2

[C]C_2 G [A]E_2 A A# A G# A

[A]A_2 E_2 [d]G_2 [d]F_2 E_2 [G]D_2

[E]E_2 B [a]C_2 [F#]A [G]G B_2 A_2

[G]G_2 F_2 E_2 F_2 A B [C]C_2

B C_2 [G]D_2 [G]E_2 D_2 [D]D_2

[D]A [F]C_2 C_2 C_2 [F]C_2 B C_2 D_2 C_2 [C]C_2

[C]G [A#]G_2 [A#]$F\#_2$ E_2 [G]D_2

[e]B [a]C_2 [D]B A B [G]G [G#]G# [C#]G#

[A]A [D]A [G]B [C]E_2 F# G

[C]G# G A B E_2 D_2 [C]D_2

[C]C_2 D_2 C_2 B C_2 D_2

$\boxed{\text{A}}$ E_2 G# A A# A D_2

$\boxed{\text{A}}$ $\text{C\#}_2$ F_2 E_2 $\text{A\#}_2$ A_2 E_2 $\boxed{\text{d}}$ G_2

$\boxed{\text{d}}$ F_2 E_2 $\boxed{\text{G}}$ D_2 $\boxed{\text{E}}$ E_2 B $\boxed{\text{a}}$ C_2

$\boxed{\text{F\#}}$ A $\boxed{\text{G}}$ G B_2 A_2 G_2 F_2 E_2 F_2 A B $\boxed{\text{C}}$ C_2

O sole mio

[C] G F E D [C] C [C] D E C [F] B A$_{-2}$

B$_{-2}$ C D [G] B$_{-2}$ A$_{-2}$ A$_{-2}$

B$_{-2}$ C D [C] A$_{-2}$ G$_{-2}$ G$_{-2}$

G F E D [C] C [C] D E C [d] B$_{-2}$ A

F E D [C] G E D C [G] D E [C] D C

[C] C$_2$ [C] C$_2$ B [C] G G B B A [G] F

B B A [d] F F D E F [C] G

G [f] G# G# F C$_2$ G# [C] G G

E D C [G] G G E D C [C] C

Pineapple Rag

A G F E D# E D C D E G

A A G# A B C_2 D_2 G G

[C] A G F E D# E D [C] C D E G

[C] A G F E D# E F [C] G G E G E G

[F] C C C_2 C C_2 C C_2

E_2 C_2 E G F# G A

[G] B G B [D] A B G

[C] A G F E D# E D [C] C D E G

[C] A G F E D# E F [C] G G E G E G

[F] C C C_2 C C_2 C C_2

E_2 C_2 E E G A C_2

[F] C_2 [G] D_2 E_2 C_2 G F# G G# A A#

47

[G] B B$_2$ A A$_2$ B B$_2$ A$_2$ B$_2$ A$_2$

[C] A A$_2$ G G$_2$ A A$_2$ G$_2$ A$_2$ G$_2$

[G] G G$_2$ F F$_2$ E E$_2$ F$_2$ E$_2$ D$_2$

[C] D D$_2$ D C$_2$ A

[C] G G F# G G# A A#

[G] B B$_2$ A A$_2$ B B$_2$ A$_2$ B$_2$ A$_2$

[C] A A$_2$ G G$_2$ A A$_2$ G$_2$ A$_2$ G$_2$

[f] G# F$_2$ C$_2$ G# **[C]** G C$_2$ F# G

[G] F D$_2$ E$_2$ D$_2$ **[C]** C$_2$ C D E F G

[C] A G F E D# E D **[C]** C D E G

[C] A G F E D# E F **[C]** G G E G E G

[F] C C$_2$ C C$_2$ C C$_2$ E$_2$

C$_2$ E G F# G A

$\boxed{\text{G}}$ B G B $\boxed{\text{D}}$ A B G

$\boxed{\text{C}}$ A G F E D# E D $\boxed{\text{C}}$ C D E G

$\boxed{\text{C}}$ A G F E D# E F $\boxed{\text{C}}$ G G E G E G

$\boxed{\text{F}}$ C C_2 C C_2 C C_2

E_2 C_2 E E G A C_2

$\boxed{\text{F}}$ C_2 $\boxed{\text{G}}$ D_2 E_2 C_2 C_3

Por Una Cabeza

E F F# G [C]A G F# G A B

[C]D₂ C₂ E₂ F₂ D₂ E₂ C

C D₂ B C₂ B G

[G]F F₂ E₂ G₂ F₂ [G]D₂ D₂ C#₂ E₂ D₂

[G]B B C₂ C#₂ D₂

[G]E₂ D₂ B G G# B A F

[C]E E F F# G [C]A G F# G A B

[C]D₂ C₂ C₂ D₂ E₂ C₂ [C]D₂ C₂ D₂ E₂ D₂ C₂

[F]A₂ D₂ C₂ A F [d]E D E F

[f]G# C₂ A# G#

[C]C₂ G C₂ D₂ E₂ C₂

[G]D₂ D₂ B C₂ D₂ B

50

C_2 $D\#_2$ $D\#_2$ F_2 G_2

G_2 D_2 C_2 C_2 D_2 $D\#_2$

$D\#_2$ $A\#$ $G\#$ $G\#$ $A\#$ C_2

C_2 G C_2 D_2 $D\#_2$ C_2

D_2 D_2 C_2 D_2 $D\#_2$ C_2

$D\#_2$ D_2 $D\#_2$ $D\#_2$ F_2 G_2

G_2 D_2 C_2 C_2 D_2 $D\#_2$

$D\#_2$ $A\#$ $G\#$ $G\#$ $A\#$ C_2

C_2 G C_2 D_2 $D\#_2$ C_2

D_2 D_2 B C_2 D_2 B C_2

Radetzky March

[C] C_2 C_2 C_2 C_2 C_2 C_2 E_2 D_2 C_2

B [D]A G# A B C_2 D_2 [G]G

E_2 $D\#_2$ [C]E_2 E_2 $D\#_2$ E_2 E_2 $D\#_2$ E_2 D_2 C_2

E_2 $D\#_2$ [C]E_2 E_2 $D\#_2$ E_2 E_2 $D\#_2$ E_2 A_2 G_2

G_2 E_2 [G]F_2 A_2 G_2 G_2 D_2 [C]E_2 A_2 G_2

G_2 E_2 [D]D_2 B_2 C_2 A_2 [G]B

G_2 $F\#_2$ G_2 A_2 G_2 F_2

[C]E_2 E_2 $D\#_2$ E_2 E_2 $D\#_2$ E_2 D_2 C_2 E_2 $D\#_2$ [C]E_2

E_2 $D\#_2$ E_2 E_2 $D\#_2$ E_2 A_2 G_2

G_2 E_2 [D]$F\#_2$ E_3 D_3 [C]D_3 C_3

[G]B_2 A_2 G_2 F_2 E_2 D_2 [C]C_2 C_3 C_2

Moonlight Sonata

[d] A_{-2} D F A_{-2} D F A_{-2} D F A_{-2} D F

[d] A_{-2} D F A_{-2} D F A_{-2} D F A_{-2} D F

[A#] $A\#_{-2}$ D F $A\#_{-2}$ D F [g] $A\#_{-2}$ D# G $A\#_{-2}$ D# G

[A] A_{-2} C# G [d] A_{-2} D F [d] A_{-2} D E [A] G_{-2} C# E

[d] F_{-2} A_{-2} D A_{-2} D F [d] A_{-2} D F A A

[A] A E G A_{-2} E G [A] A_{-2} E G A A

[d] A D F A_{-2} D F [g] A# D G $A\#_{-2}$ D G

[F] A C F A_{-2} C F [C] G C E C_{2} C E

[F] F C F A_{-2} C F A_{-2} C F A_{-2} C F

[f] $G\#_{-2}$ C F $G\#_{-2}$ C F [f] $G\#_{-2}$ C F G# G#

[G#] G# C F# $G\#_{-2}$ C F# [G#] $G\#_{-2}$ C F# G# G#

[C#] G# C# F $G\#_{-2}$ C F [d#] $G\#_{-2}$ D F G D F

[c] G C D# G_{-2} C D# [f] G# C D F C D

[c] G C D# G_{-2} C D# [G] G B_{-2} D G B_{-2} D

[c] C D# G C D# G [C] C E G C_2 E G

Swan Lake

[a]E$_2$ [d]A B C$_2$ D$_2$ [a]E$_2$ C$_2$ E$_2$ C$_2$

[a]E$_2$ A [F]C$_2$ A F C$_2$ [a]A D$_2$ C$_2$ B

[a]E$_2$ [d]A B C$_2$ D$_2$ [a]E$_2$ C$_2$ E$_2$ C$_2$

[a]E$_2$ A [F]C$_2$ A F C$_2$ [a]A A$_{-2}$

[G]B$_{-2}$ C D E F [e]G F E F G

[d]A G F G A [B]B A E C [E]B$_{-2}$ [a]A$_{-2}$

[G]B$_{-2}$ C D E F [e]G F E F G

[d]A G F [F]G A [A#]A# F D F A#

[B]B F# [E]B E [a]E$_2$ [d]A B C$_2$ D$_2$

[a]E$_2$ C$_2$ E$_2$ C$_2$ [a]E$_2$ A [F]C$_2$ A F C$_2$ [a]A

D$_2$ C$_2$ B [a]E$_2$ A B C$_2$ D$_2$

[a]E$_2$ C$_2$ E$_2$ C$_2$ [a]E$_2$ A [d]C$_2$ A F C$_2$ [a]A

Tarantella napoletana

A_2 A_2 [a] E_2 E_2 A_2 A_2

E_2 E_2 E_2 [d] F_2 F_2 F_2 G_2 F_2

[a] E_2 E_2 E_2 [E] E_2 D_2 D_2 D_2

[a] D_2 C_2 C_2 C_2 [E] C_2 B B C_2 B

[a] A A_2 A_2 [a] E_2 E_2 A_2 A_2

E_2 E_2 E_2 [d] F_2 F_2 F_2 G_2 F_2

[a] E_2 E_2 E_2 [E] E_2 D_2 D_2 D_2

[a] D_2 C_2 C_2 C_2 [E] C_2 B B C_2 B

[a] A A B [a] C_2 B C_2 [d] D_2 C_2 B

[a] C_2 B C_2 [d] D_2 C_2 B [a] C_2 B A $G\#$ A [E] B

[a] A A B [a] C_2 B C_2 [d] D_2 C_2 D_2

[a] E_2 D_2 E_2 [d] F_2 E_2 D_2 [a] C_2 B A $G\#$ A [E] B

[a] A A B [a] C_2 B C_2 [d] D_2 C_2 B

[a] C_2 B C_2 [d] D_2 C_2 B

[a] C_2 B A [E] G# A B [a] A

The Entertainer

D_2 E_2 C_2 A B G D E C A_{-2} B_{-2} G_{-2}

D E C A_{-2} B_{-2} A_{-2} $G\#_{-2}$ $\boxed{G}$ G_{-2} G

D D# $\boxed{C}$ E C_2 E C_2 E C_2 $\boxed{F}$

C_2 D_2 $D\#_2$ $\boxed{C}$ E_2 C_2 D_2 E_2 $\boxed{G}$ B D_2 $\boxed{C}$ C_2

D D# $\boxed{C}$ E C_2 E C_2 E C_2 $\boxed{F}$

A G $\boxed{D}$ F# A C_2 E_2 D_2 C_2 A $\boxed{G}$ D_2

D D# $\boxed{C}$ E C_2 E C_2 E C_2 $\boxed{F}$

C_2 D_2 $D\#_2$ $\boxed{C}$ E_2 C_2 D_2 E_2 $\boxed{G}$ B D_2 $\boxed{C}$ C_2

C_2 D_2 $\boxed{C}$ E_2 C_2 D_2 E_2

$\boxed{C}$ C_2 D_2 C_2 $\boxed{F}$ E_2 C_2 D_2 E $\boxed{f}$

C_2 D_2 C_2 $\boxed{C}$ E_2 C_2 D_2 E_2 $\boxed{G}$ B D_2 $\boxed{C}$ C_2

Trisch – trasch polka

$\boxed{G}$ B A B $\boxed{C}$ C$_2$ G $\boxed{C}$ G$_2$ G G$_2$ F#$_2$

$\boxed{C}$ F$_2$ E$_2$ D$_2$ C$_2$ $\boxed{G}$ B

A $\boxed{G}$ D$_2$ A D$_2$ F# $\boxed{G}$ G A B C$_2$ D$_2$ $\boxed{C}$ E$_2$

G $\boxed{C}$ G$_2$ G G$_2$ F#$_2$ $\boxed{C}$ F$_2$ E$_2$ D$_2$ C$_2$ $\boxed{G}$ B

B $\boxed{A}$ E$_2$ B E$_2$ A$_{-2}$ B$_{-2}$ $\boxed{A}$ C# E G C#$_2$ $\boxed{D}$ D$_2$

D$_2$ $\boxed{G}$ B$_2$ B$_2$ B$_2$ A$_2$ G$_2$ $\boxed{C}$ C$_3$ C$_3$ C$_2$

$\boxed{G}$ B$_2$ B$_2$ B $\boxed{C}$ A$_2$ A$_2$ G$_2$ G$_2$ G$_2$

$\boxed{G}$ B$_2$ B$_2$ B$_2$ A$_2$ G$_2$ $\boxed{C}$ C$_3$ C$_3$ C$_2$

C$_2$ D$_2$ D#$_2$ D#$_2$ D$_2$ C$_2$

Vivaldi Four Seasons: Autumn

[C] E_2 E_2 E_2 F_2 E_2 E_2 F_2

[C] E_2 E_2 E_2 F_2 E_2 E_2 F_2

[C] E_2 D_2 E_2 [d] F_2 E_2 [G] D_2

[C] E E E F E E F

[C] E E F E E F [C] E D E [d] F E [G] D

[C] E_2 E_2 E_2 G_2 [d] A A A

[G] D_2 D_2 D_2 F_2 [C] G G C_2

[C] E_2 E_2 E_2 F_2 [C] E_2 E_2 E_2 F_2

[C] E_2 E_2 E_2 F_2 E_2 D_2 E_2 [G] F_2 D_2

[C] E_2 [C] E_2 E_2 E_2 F_2

E_2 E_2 E_2 F_2 [C] E_2 E_2 E_2 F_2

[C] E_2 D_2 E_2 [G] F_2 D_2 [C] C_2

[C] E_2 E_2 E_2 F_2 E_2 E_2 F_2

[C] E_2 E_2 E_2 F_2 E_2 E_2 F_2

[C] E_2 [d] D_2 E_2 F_2 E_2 [G] D_2

[C] E E F E E F [C] E E E F E E F

[C] E D E F E [d] D [G] [C] C_2

G G G [F] A [C] G G

[C] C_2 G G G [F] A [C] G G [F] A

[C] G G [C] C_2 B A G F

[C] E [G] D [C] C [C] C_3 G_2 G_2 G_2 [F] A_2 [C] G_2 G_2

[C] C_3 G_2 G_2 G_2 [F] A_2 [C] G_2 G_2 [F] A_2 [C] G_2 G_2 [C] C_3 G_2 A_2 G_2 F_2

[C] E_2 [G] D_2 [C] C_2 E_2 E_2 F_2

[C] E_2 E_2 E_2 F_2 [C] E_2 E_2 E_2 F_2

[C] E_2 [G] D_2 E_2 F_2 D_2 [C] E_2

$\boxed{C}$ E E F $\boxed{C}$ E E F $\boxed{C}$ E E F

$\boxed{C}$ E D E $\boxed{G}$ F D

$\boxed{C}$ E $\boxed{C}$ C C_2 G E $\boxed{C}$ C C_2 G E

$\boxed{C}$ C C E G

$\boxed{C}$ C_2 $\boxed{C}$ C_2 G E $\boxed{C}$ C E G $\boxed{C}$ C_2 E_2 $\boxed{a}$ A_2 A $\boxed{d}$ D_2 E_2 F_2 $\boxed{G}$ G_2 G

$\boxed{C}$ C_2 D_2 E_2 F_2 $\boxed{F}$ F B $\boxed{G}$ C_2 D_2 $\boxed{e}$ E_2 E

$\boxed{a}$ A B C_2 $\boxed{d}$ D_2 D $\boxed{G}$ G A B $\boxed{C}$ C_2 C

$\boxed{C}$ E E F $\boxed{C}$ E C D E F

G A B $\boxed{C}$ C_2 E_2 E_2 F_2

$\boxed{C}$ E_2 E_2 E_2 F_2 $\boxed{C}$ E_2 E_2 E_2 F_2

$\boxed{C}$ E_2 D_2 E_2 F_2 $\boxed{G}$ D_2 $\boxed{C}$ E_2

$\boxed{C}$ E E F $\boxed{C}$ E E F $\boxed{C}$ E E F

$\boxed{C}$ E D E F $\boxed{G}$ D $\boxed{C}$ C

Vivaldi Four Seasons: Spring

C_2 [C]$\overset{}{E}_2$ E_2 E_2 D_2 C_2 G_2 G_2 F_2

[C]$\overset{}{E}_2$ E_2 E_2 D_2 C_2 G_2 G_2 F_2

[C]$\overset{}{E}_2$ F_2 G_2 [F]$\overset{}{F}_2$ E_2 D_2 [G]B G C_2

[C]$\overset{}{E}_2$ E_2 E_2 D_2 C_2 G_2 G_2 F_2

[C]$\overset{}{E}_2$ E_2 E_2 D_2 C_2 G_2 G_2 F_2

[C]$\overset{}{E}_2$ F_2 G_2 [F]$\overset{}{F}_2$ E_2 [G]D_2 E_2

[C]$\overset{}{G}_2$ F_2 E_2 [F]$\overset{}{F}_2$ G_2 [C]$\overset{}{A}_2$ G_2 E_2

[C]$\overset{}{G}_2$ F_2 E_2 [F]$\overset{}{F}_2$ G_2 [C]$\overset{}{A}_2$ G_2 E_2

[C]$\overset{}{A}_2$ G_2 F_2 [C]$\overset{}{E}_2$ D_2 C_2 [G]$\overset{}{D}_2$

[C]$\overset{}{C}_2$ E_2 [C]$\overset{}{G}_2$ F_2 E_2 [F]$\overset{}{F}_2$ G_2 [C]$\overset{}{A}_2$ G_2 E_2

[C]$\overset{}{G}_2$ F_2 E_2 [F]$\overset{}{F}_2$ G_2

[C]$\overset{}{A}_2$ G_2 E_2 [C]$\overset{}{A}_2$ G_2 F_2

63

[C] E_2 D_2 C_2 [G] D_2 [C] C_2

[C] F_2 E_2 F_2 E_2 F_2 E_2 F_2 E_2

[C] G_2 G_2 G_2 G_2 G_2 G_2 G_2 G_2 G_2

[C] G_2 G_2 G_2 G_2 [G] G_2 G_2 G_2 A_2 B_2

[C] C_3 B_2 A_2 G_2 F_2 E_2 D_2 C_2 C_3 C_3 C_3 C_3

[C] C_2 C_3 C_3 C_3 C_3 C_3

[C] C_2 G_2 C_3 G_2 A_2 [C] G_2 C_3 G_2 A_2 G_2 A_2

G_2 C_3 G_2 A_2 G_2 C_3 G_2 A_2

[C] G_2 C_3 G_2 A_2 G_2 C_3 G_2 A_2 G_2 C_2 E_2

[C] E_2 F_2 E_2 E_2 F_2 E_2

[C] E_2 F_2 E_2 C_2 C_3

[C] C_3 D_3 C_3 D_3 C_3 D_3 C_3 D_3 C_2 C_3

[C] C_3 D_3 C_3 D_3 C_3 D_3 C_3 D_3 C_3 E_2

$\boxed{C}$ G_2 F_2 E_2 F_2 $\boxed{F}$ G_2 A_2 $\boxed{C}$ G_2 E_2

$\boxed{C}$ G_2 F_2 E_2 F_2 $\boxed{F}$ G_2 A_2 $\boxed{C}$ G_2 E_2

$\boxed{C}$ A_2 G_2 F_2 $\boxed{C}$ E_2 D_2 C_2 $\boxed{G}$ D_2

$\boxed{C}$ C_2 E_2 $\boxed{C}$ G_2 F_2 E_2 $\boxed{F}$ F_2 G_2

$\boxed{C}$ A_2 G_2 E_2 $\boxed{C}$ G_2 F_2 E_2 $\boxed{F}$ F_2 G_2

$\boxed{C}$ A_2 G_2 E_2 $\boxed{C}$ A_2 G_2 F_2

$\boxed{C}$ E_2 D_2 C_2 $\boxed{G}$ D_2 $\boxed{C}$ C_2

Vivaldi Four Seasons: Winter

[C] C$_2$ G$_2$ F$_2$ E$_2$ D$_2$ C$_2$ [G] D$_2$ G G

[G] F$_2$ E$_2$ D$_2$ C$_2$ B F$_2$ [C] F$_2$ E$_2$ E$_2$

[G] D$_2$ E$_2$ F$_2$ G$_2$ A$_2$ G$_2$

C D$_2$ E$_2$ [d] F$_2$ G$_2$ A$_2$

[G] B C$_2$ D$_2$ [C] E$_2$ F$_2$ G$_2$

[F] A B C$_2$ [D] D$_2$ E$_2$ C$_2$

[G] B G F# G [G] D$_2$ G F# G

[C] E$_2$ G F# G [D] F# D$_2$ C$_2$ D$_2$

[G] G$_2$ G G$_2$ [D] G$_2$ F#$_2$ E$_2$ D$_2$

C$_2$ B A G [D] A G [G] G

[G] G D$_2$ C$_2$ B A G [D] A D D

[D] C$_2$ B A G F# C$_2$ [G] C$_2$ B G

[G] F$_2$ E$_2$ D$_2$ C$_2$ B F$_2$ [C] F$_2$ E$_2$ E$_2$

[F]
$A \ B \ C_2 \ D_2 \ E_2 \ F_2$

[G]
$B \ C_2 \ D_2 \ E_2 \ F_2 \ G_2$

[a] [G]
$C_2 \ D_2 \ E_2 \ F_2 \ G_2 \ A_2 \ B \ B \ C_2$

[G] [C]
$D_2 \ B \ A \ G \ E_2 \ F_2 \ G_2 \ E_2$

[G]
$D_2 \ G \ B \ C_2$

[G] [C]
$D_2 \ B \ A \ G \ E_2 \ F_2 \ G_2 \ E_2$

[G]
$D_2 \ G \ D_2 \ G_2$

[C] [G] [C]
$E_2 \ D_2 \ C_2 \ B \ C_2 \ C_2$

Wilhelm Tell Ouverture, Rossini

[C] G G G G G

[C] G E C E G E G C

[C] G E C E G E G C

[C] G G G G G

[C] G E C E G E G C

[G] G G G G G G G G G

[G] G G G G G G G G G G [G]

G₋₂ G₋₂ [C] G₋₂ G₋₂ G₋₂ G₋₂ G₋₂ G₋₂

C D E G₋₂ G₋₂

[C] G₋₂ G₋₂ G₋₂ C E E [G] D B₋₂ G₋₂ G₋₂ G₋₂

[C] G₋₂ G₋₂ G₋₂ G₋₂ G₋₂ G₋₂ C D E C E

G F E D [C] C E C G G

[C] G G G G G G C₋₂ D₋₂ E₋₂ G G

68

[C] G G G C$_2$ E$_2$ E$_2$ [G] D$_2$ B G G G

G G G G G G C$_2$ D$_2$ E$_2$ C$_2$ E$_2$

[G] G$_2$ F$_2$ E$_2$ D$_2$ [C] C$_2$ E$_2$ C$_2$ E$_2$ E$_2$

[a] E$_2$ E$_2$ E$_2$ E$_2$ E$_2$ E$_2$ E$_2$ A$_2$ E$_2$ A$_2$

[a] E$_2$ A$_2$ E$_2$ D$_2$ [E] C$_2$ B [a] A E$_2$ E$_2$

[a] E$_2$ E$_2$ E$_2$ E$_2$ E$_2$ E$_2$ E$_2$ A$_2$ E$_2$ A$_2$

[a] E$_2$ A$_2$ [D] G$_2$ F#$_2$ [G] G$_2$ F#$_2$ G$_2$ E$_2$ E$_2$

[a] E$_2$ E$_2$ E$_2$ E$_2$ E$_2$ E$_2$ E$_2$ A$_2$ E$_2$ A$_2$

[a] E$_2$ A$_2$ E$_2$ D$_2$ [E] C$_2$ B [a] A E$_2$ E$_2$

[a] E$_2$ E$_2$ E$_2$ E$_2$ E$_2$ E$_2$ E$_2$ A$_2$ E$_2$ A$_2$

[a] E$_2$ A$_2$ [D] G$_2$ F#$_2$ [G] G$_2$ F#$_2$ G$_2$ D D

[G] D D D E F D F [C] E C E [G] D D D

[G] D D D E F D F

[C] E C E D [G] G$_{-2}$ G$_{-2}$

[C] G$_{-2}$ G$_{-2}$ G$_{-2}$ G$_{-2}$ G$_{-2}$ G$_{-2}$

C D E G$_{-2}$ G$_{-2}$

[C] G$_{-2}$ G$_{-2}$ G$_{-2}$ C E E D B$_{-2}$ [G] G$_{-2}$ G$_{-2}$ G$_{-2}$

[C] G$_{-2}$ G$_{-2}$ G$_{-2}$ G$_{-2}$ G$_{-2}$ G$_{-2}$ C D E C E

[G] G F E D [C] C E C G G [C] G G G G

G C$_2$ D$_2$ E$_2$ G G

[C] G G G C$_2$ E$_2$ E$_2$ [G] D$_2$ B G G

[C] G G G G G C$_2$ D$_2$ E$_2$ C$_2$ E$_2$

[G] G$_2$ F$_2$ E$_2$ D$_2$ [C] C$_2$ E$_2$ C$_2$

[C] C$_2$ C$_2$ C$_2$ C$_2$ E$_2$ D$_2$

[F] C$_2$ B C$_2$ A [C] G F# G C$_2$

[G] F E F A [a] E D E G

70

[G] D C# D F [C] C D E G

[C] C_2 C_2 C_2 C_2 E_2 D_2

[F] C_2 B C_2 A [C] G F# G C_2

[G] F E F A [a] E D E G

[G] D C# D G [C] C

Ode to Joy

[C] E E F G [G] G F E D

Joy, beautiful spark of gods,

[C] C C D E [G] E D D

Daughter of Elysium,

[C] E E F G [G] G F E D

We enter, drunk with fire,

[C] C C D E [G] D C [C] C

Heavenly one, thy sanctuary!

[G] D D E [C] C D [G] E F [C] E C

Thy magic binds again

[G] D E F E [E] D C [a] D [G] G$_{-2}$

What custom strictly divided;*

[C] E E F G [G] G F E D

All people become brothers,*

[C] C C D E [G] D C [C] C

Where thy gentle wing abides.

500 miles away from home

C$_2$ D$_2$ [d] D$_2$ E$_2$ D$_2$ [G] C$_2$ A C$_2$ C$_2$ [C]

I'm 500 miles away from home

A C$_2$ E$_2$ [C] E$_2$ [G] D$_2$ C$_2$ E$_2$

Teardrops fell on mama's note

A C$_2$ E$_2$ [C] E$_2$ [G] D$_2$ C$_2$ A

When I read the things she wrote

G A C$_2$ D$_2$ [d] D$_2$ E$_2$

She said, „We miss you son

E$_2$ D$_2$ [F] C$_2$ A C$_2$ D$_2$ [G]

We love you, come on home"

A C$_2$ E$_2$ [C] E$_2$ [G] D$_2$ C$_2$ E$_2$

Well I didn't have to pack

A C$_2$ D$_2$ E$_2$ [C] E$_2$ [G] D$_2$ C$_2$ A

I had it all right on my back

A C$_2$ D$_2$ [d] D$_2$ E$_2$ [F] D$_2$ C$_2$ A C$_2$ D$_2$ [G]

Now I'm 500 miles away from home

73

1812 Overture

[C] G C_2 D_2 E_2 D_2 C_2 D_2 E_2 C_2 C_2

[C] G C_2 D_2 E_2 D_2 C_2 D_2 E_2 C_2 C_2

[D] A D_2 E_2 D_2 A G A D_2 E_2 D_2 A D_2

[C] G C_2 D_2 C_2 G E G C_2 D_2 C_2 G C_2

[C] G C_2 D_2 E_2 D_2 C_2 D_2 E_2 C_2 C_2

[C] G C_2 D_2 E_2 D_2 C_2 D_2 E_2 C_2 C_2

[D] A D_2 E_2 D_2 A G A D_2 E_2 D_2 A D_2

[C] G C_2 D_2 C_2 G E G C_2 D_2 C_2 G C_2

[C] G C_2 D_2 E_2 D_2 C_2 D_2 E_2 C_2 C_2

[C] G C_2 D_2 E_2 D_2 C_2 D_2 E_2 C_2 C_2

Air on a G string

[C] E_2 [a] E_2 A_2 F_2 D_2 C_2 B_2 C_2

[G] B A G [e] G_2 [A] G_2 E_2 A# A

D_2 C# G_2 F_2 [d] F_2

[G] F_2 D_2 A G C_2 B F_2 E_2 [C] E_2

F# G_2 [a] C_2 C_2 D_2 E_2 E_2 D_2 D_2 C_2

[G] B A A B C_2 C_2 B A [G] G [C] E_2 [a] E_2

A_2 F_2 D_2 C_2 B C_2 [G] B A G

[e] G_2 [A] G_2 E_2 A# A D_2 C# G_2 F_2

[d] F_2 [G] F_2 D_2 A G C_2 B F_2 E_2

[C] E_2 F# G_2 [a] C_2 C_2 D_2 E_2 E_2 D_2 D_2 C_2

[G] B A A B C_2 C_2 B A [G] G

Bridal chorus from Lohengrin Wagner

[C]
G C_2 C_2 C_2 [G]G D_2 B [C]C_2

[C]
G C_2 F_2 [F]F_2 E_2 D_2

[C]
C_2 B C_2 [G]D_2 [C]G C_2 C_2 C_2

[G]
G D_2 B [C]C_2 [C]G C_2 E_2 G_2 E_2 C_2

[F] [G]
A D_2 E_2 [C]C_2

Caprice Number 24

[a] A A A C_2 B A [E] E_2 E E G# F# E

[a] A A A C_2 B A [E] E_2 E

[a] A A A C_2 B A [E] E_2 E E G# F# E

[a] A A A C_2 B A [E] E_2 E

[a] A_2 A_2 A_2 B_2 A_2 G_2

[d] F_2 D_2 D_2 F_2 E_2 D_2

[G] G_2 G_2 G_2 A_2 G_2 F_2

[C] E_2 C_2 C_2 E_2 D_2 C_2

[d] F_2 B B D_2 C_2 B [a] E_2 A A C_2 B A

[d] F D# [E] E_2 E_2 D_2 B [a] A

Carnival of Venice

[C] G_2 A_2 G_2 F_2 E_2

[G] F_2 D_2 D_2 E_2 F_2 A_2 G_2

[C] E_2 G_2 C_2 G_2 F_2 E_2

[G] F_2 D_2 D_2 E_2 F_2 A_2 G_2

[C] C_2 G A G F E

[G] F D D E F A G

[C] E G C_2 G F E

[G] F D D E F A G

[C] C [C] G_2 [G] C_2 G_2

[C] C_2 [G] G_2 [C] C_2 [G] G_2 [C] C_2

Die Fledermaus

[G] G F# G A G F E D# E F E D

[C] C E G A [A] A

[a] A G# A C₂ B A [d] F F F

[a] A G# A C₂ B A [e] E E E

[G] G F# G A G F E D# E F E D

[C] C E G A [E] B

[E] B A# B E₂ D# C# [A] A A A

[B] A G# A C# B D# [E] E

[G] G F# G A G F E D# E F E D

[C] C E G A [A] A

[a] A G# A C₂ B A [d] F F F

[a] A G# A C₂ B A [e] E E E

[G] G F# G A G F E D# E F E D

79

[C] C E G A [A] A

[a] A G# A C$_2$ B A [G] G G G

[d] D C# D F E D [C] C

80

Gavotte

[C] G_2 A_2 G_2 E_2 F_2 G_2 F_2 C_2 C_2 C_2

[G] F_2 G_2 F_2 D_2 E_2 F_2 E_2 C_2 D_2 G_2 G_2

[C] G_2 A_2 G_2 E_2 F_2 G_2 F_2 D_2 C_2 C_2 C_2

[a] E_2 C_2 A C_2 A F# [D] G G_2 [G] G

[d] D_2 F_2 E_2 G_2 F_2 E_2 D_2 C_2 B [G] D_2 F_2

[C] E_2 G_2 F_2 A_2 [G] G_2 F_2 E_2 D_2 [C] C_2 E_2 G_2

[a] A_2 G_2 G_2 F_2 F_2 E_2 E_2 D_2 [d] D_2 F_2 A_2

[C] G_2 E_2 B C_2 [d] F_2 D_2 A B [C] C_2 C_2 C_2

Gymnopedie

E_2 G_2 [F] F_2 E_2 B A B C_2 [C] G

E_2 G_2 [F] F_2 E_2 B A B C_2 [C] G

[g] G A B D_2 C_2 A [d] C_2 B A [c] C_2

C_2 [g] D_2 D# F_2

G_2 B C_2 D_2 C_2 A [c] C_2 C_2

[d] F_2 [e] E_2 [a] A G A B [G] C_2 D_2

B C_2 D_2 [e] E B [g] C_2 [C] E_2 G_2

[F] F_2 E_2 B A B C_2 [C] G

Hungarian Dance

[a] E A C$_2$ A [d] G# A B [a] A [d] F G A [a] E

[E] D C C B$_{-2}$ B$_{-2}$ E A$_{-2}$ [a] E A C$_2$ [a] A

[d] G# A B [a] A [F] F$_2$ G$_2$ A$_2$ F$_2$ [C] E$_2$ F$_2$ G$_2$ E$_2$

[d] D$_2$ E$_2$ F$_2$ D$_2$ C$_2$ D$_2$ [a] E$_2$ C$_2$

[E] D$_2$ C$_2$ C$_2$ B B E$_2$ [a] A

[a] E A C$_2$ A D# A B [a] A

[d] F G A E D C C B$_{-2}$ [a] B$_{-2}$ E [a] A$_{-2}$

[a] E A C$_2$ A G# A B [a] A

[F] F G$_2$ A$_2$ F$_2$ [C] E$_2$ F$_2$ G$_2$ E$_2$ [d] D$_2$ E$_2$ F$_2$ D$_2$

[a] C$_2$ D$_2$ E$_2$ C$_2$ [E] D$_2$ C$_2$ C$_2$ B B E$_2$ [a] A

[a] E$_2$ E$_2$ [d] F$_2$ E$_2$

Intermezzo No. 1

G $\boxed{C}$C$_2$ B A G F E

D C E G A B $\boxed{C}$C$_2$ B A G F E

$\boxed{G}$G C D $\boxed{C}$C E G E$_2$ $\boxed{d}$F$_2$ D$_2$ E$_2$ G

$\boxed{d}$F$_2$ D$_2$ E$_2$ E $\boxed{G}$D$_2$ G$_2$ F#

E$_2$ D$_2$ C$_2$ B D$_2$ G $\boxed{C}$C$_2$ B A G F E

D C E G A B $\boxed{C}$C$_2$ B A G F E

$\boxed{G}$G C D $\boxed{C}$C

Jimbo's Lullaby

[C] G E G A D E G EE D

[C] D E E D G E[C] D B$_{-2}$

[a] A$_{-2}$ G$_{-2}$ A$_{-2}$ B$_{-2}$ D

A$_{-2}$ E D B$_{-2}$ [a] A$_{-2}$ G$_{-2}$ A$_{-2}$ B$_{-2}$ D

A$_{-2}$ [a] A E A E A E A E

[C] G E G A D E G E D

[C] D E E D G E

D$_2$ B [a] A G A B D$_2$

A E$_2$ D$_2$ B [a] A G A B D$_2$ A

Largo

[C] E G G E D C [d] D E G E [G] D

[C] E G G E D C [d] D E D C [C] C

[F] A C₂ [G] C₂ B G [a] A

A [G] B G [a] A [F] C₂ C₂ B G [G] A [a] A

A [G] C₂ B G [a] A

[C] E G G E D C

[d] D E G E D [G] E [C] G G

[a] C₂ [F] D₂ E₂ [F] D₂ C₂ D₂ A [C] C₂

[F] D₂ C₂ D₂ A [C] C₂

[F] D₂ C₂ [d] D₂ A [C] C₂

86

Minuet in D Minor Bach

[a]
$\overset{}{E}$ C$_2$ B A G# A E F

[E]
G# B$_{-2}$ D F E D [a] C B$_{-2}$ C A$_{-2}$

[a]
C F E A G [C] C$_2$ B A G F

[F]
E F G C [G] B$_{-2}$ [C] C

[a]
E C$_2$ B A G# A E F

[E]
G# B$_{-2}$ D F E D

[a]
C B$_2$ C A$_{-2}$

[a]
C F E A G [C] C$_2$ B A G F

[F]
E F G C [G] B$_{-2}$ [C] C

[C]
E$_2$ C E$_2$ D$_2$ C$_2$ B C$_2$ D$_2$ G

[a]
C$_2$ A$_{-2}$ C$_2$ B A G# A B E

[a]
E F# G# A B C$_2$ D$_2$ B$_2$ G# F$_2$ E$_2$ D$_2$

[d]
C$_2$ B A B$_2$ [E] G# [a] A

$\boxed{C}$ E_2 C E_2 D_2 C_2 B C_2 D_2 G

$\boxed{a}$ C_2 A_2 C_2 B A G# A B

$\boxed{a}$ E F# G# A B C_2 $\boxed{E}$ D_2 B G# F_2 E_2 D_2

$\boxed{d}$ C B A B $\boxed{E}$ G# $\boxed{a}$ A

Morning from Peer Gynt

[F] C₂ A G F G A [F] C₂ A G F G A G A

[F] C₂ A C₂ [d] D₂ A D₂ [F] C₂ A G F

[F] C₂ A G F G A [F] C₂ A G F G A G A

[F] C₂ A C₂ [d] D₂ A D₂ [A] E₂ C# B A

[A] E₂ C# B A B C# [A] E₂ C# B A B C# B C#

[A] E₂ C# [f#] E₂ F# C# F# [A] E₂ C# B A

[A] E₂ C# B A B C# [A] E₂ C# B A B C# B C#

[A] E₂ C# E₂ F₂ D₂ F₂ [C] G₂ E₂ D₂ C₂

Over the Waves

$\boxed{\text{C}}$
E D# E G $\boxed{\text{C}}$ C$_2$ B C$_2$

$\boxed{\text{C}}$
D$_2$ C$_2$ B C$_2$ E G $\boxed{\text{G}}$ B

$\boxed{\text{G}}$
F E F G $\boxed{\text{G}}$ B A# B

$\boxed{\text{G}}$
C$_2$ B A# B F B $\boxed{\text{C}}$ E

$\boxed{\text{C}}$
E D# E G $\boxed{\text{C}}$ C$_2$ B C$_2$

$\boxed{\text{C}}$
D$_2$ C$_2$ B C$_2$ E A

$\boxed{\text{F}}$ $\boxed{\text{A}}$ $\boxed{\text{d}}$
A A A D$_2$ F$_2$ A$_2$

$\boxed{\text{C}}$ $\boxed{\text{G}}$
G$_2$ F$_2$ E$_2$ D$_2$ C$_2$ B A B D$_2$

$\boxed{\text{C}}$
C$_2$

Piano Sonata No. 11

[C] E_2 F_2 E_2 G_2 G_2 [G] D_2 E_2 D_2 F_2 F_2

[C] C_2 C_2 D_2 D_2 E_2 G_2 F_2 E_2 D_2

[C] E_2 F_2 E_2 G_2 G_2 [G] D_2 E_2 D_2 F_2 F_2

[C] C_2 D_2 E_2 F_2 E_2 D_2 C_2

[C] E_2 F_2 E_2 G_2 G_2 [G] D_2 E_2 D_2 F_2 F_2

[C] C_2 C_2 D_2 D_2 E_2 G_2 F_2 E_2 D_2

[C] E_2 F_2 E_2 G_2 G_2 [G] D_2 E_2 D_2 F_2 F_2

[C] C_2 D_2 E_2 F_2 E_2 D_2 C_2

Prelude G major Chopin

G $\overset{\boxed{G}}{E}_2$ F$_2$ D$_2$ D$_2$ D$_2$ A$_2$ $\overset{\boxed{C}}{F}$# G$_2$ C$_2$ C$_2$

C$_2$ E$_2$ $\overset{\boxed{G}}{C}$# D$_2$ F$_2$ F$_2$ F$_2$ B $\overset{\boxed{C}}{B}$ C$_2$ E$_2$ E$_2$

E$_2$ G $\overset{\boxed{G}}{E}_2$ F$_2$ D$_2$ D$_2$ D$_2$ A$_2$ $\overset{\boxed{C}}{F}$# G$_2$ E$_2$ E$_2$

E$_2$ E$_2$ $\overset{\boxed{d}}{E}_2$ F$_2$ A$_2$ A$_2$ A$_2$ B $\overset{\boxed{G}}{D}_2$ $\overset{\boxed{C}}{C}_2$ C$_2$ C$_2$ C$_2$

Triumphal March Verdi

G [C] C_2 D_2 G D_2 E_2 E_2 E_2 E_2 F_2 C_2

[G] E_2 [C] D_2 [G] C_2 D_2 E_2 E_2 D_2 [C] C_2

D_2 E_2 E_2 D_2 E_2 E_2 C_2 D_2 [G] D_2 A A A A

B [C] C_2 D_2 G D_2 E_2 E_2 E_2 E_2 F_2 C_2

[G] E_2 [C] D_2 [G] C_2 D_2 E_2 E_2 D_2 [C] C_2

D_2 E_2 E_2 D_2 E_2 E_2 C_2 D_2

[C] C_2 C_2 G C_2 [G] D_2 G_2 G_2

C_2 G C_2 [G] D_2 G G C_2 G C_2 [G] D_2

G_2 G_2 G_2 D_2 D_2

The Swan

C$_3$ B$_2$ E$_2$ [a]A$_2$ G$_2$ C$_2$ [d]D$_2$ E$_2$ F$_2$

[d]A B C$_2$ [G]D$_2$ E$_2$ F$_2$ G$_2$ A$_2$ B$_2$

[C]E$_3$ [C]C$_3$ B$_2$ E$_2$ [a]A$_2$ G$_2$ C$_2$

[B]D# E$_2$ F# [B]B C# D# E$_2$

F# G$_2$ A$_2$ B$_2$ C# D#

[e]G$_3$ [C]C$_3$ B$_2$ E$_2$ [a]A$_2$ G$_2$ C$_2$

[d]D$_2$ E$_2$ F$_2$ [d]A B C$_2$ [G]D$_2$ E$_2$

F$_2$ G$_2$ A$_2$ B$_2$ [C]E$_3$ [d]E$_3$ D$_3$ A$_2$

C$_3$ B$_2$ F$_2$ [a]A$_2$ G$_2$ C$_2$ D$_2$ E$_2$ C$_2$

[a]E$_2$ [F]F$_2$ G$_2$ E$_2$ [a]A$_2$ [G]A$_2$ B$_2$ G$_2$ [C]C$_3$ C$_3$

Tales of Hoffmann

[D] F# G G F# [A] F# E G G F#

[A] F# E G G F# [D] F# B B A

[D] F# G G F# [A] F# E G G F#

[A] F# E G G F# [D] F# B B A

[D] A B B C# [A] C# D_2 D_2 C#

[A] C# B B A A F# D_2 A

D B B C# [A] C# D_2 D_2 C#

[A] C# B B A [D] A B B A

Symphony no.94 ‚Surprise' Haydn

[C] C C E E G G E [G] F F D D B_{-2} B_{-2} G_{-2}

[C] C C E E G G E [D] C_2 C_2 F# F# [G] G [G] G

F E [D] D D E F G A G F E [D] D D D#

[C] E E G G C_2 C_2 E_2 [G] D_2 D_2 C_2 B A B

[C] C_2 C_2 C_2

Symphony no. 9

[e]
E F E F [e]E F E F

[a]
E₂ F₂ E₂ F# E₂ G# E₂ A₂

[e]
E₂ B₂ E₂ C₃ E₂ D₃ E₂ D#

[e]
E₃ F₃ E₃ F₃ E₃ F# E₃ G#

[a]A B C₂ [d]B A A [a]A [e]G E G

[a]A A [a]A B C₂ [d]B A A [a]A C₂

A B [E]E [a]A [a]A B C₂

[d]B A A [a]A [e]G E G [a]A A

[a]A B C₂ [d]B A A [a]A C₂ A

[E]B E [a]A

Symphony No. 5

E E E [a]C D D D [E]B$_{-2}$

E E E [a]C F F F E C$_2$ C$_2$ C$_2$

[a]A E E E [E]B$_{-2}$ F F F E D$_2$ D$_2$ D$_2$

[E]B E$_2$ E$_2$ D$_2$ [a]C$_2$ [E]B E$_2$ E$_2$ D$_2$

[a]C$_2$ [E]B E$_2$ E$_2$ D$_2$ [a]C$_2$ [d]A$_2$ [a]E$_2$

Song of Toreador from Carmen

[C]
G A G E E E D E F E

[F]   [C]
F D G E C A_{-2} D G_{-2}

[d]
D A G F E D E F E

[e]   [B]
B_{-2} E E D# F# B

[a]
A G# A D E F [C] E C A G

[C]   [G]   [C]
C G_{-2} F E D C

Scotland the brave

$\boxed{C}$
C C D E C E G C$_2$ C$_2$ B C$_2$ G E C

$\boxed{F}$ $\boxed{C}$ $\boxed{G}$
F A F E G E C D G G G

$\boxed{C}$
C C D E C E G C$_2$ C$_2$ B C$_2$ G E C

$\boxed{F}$ $\boxed{C}$ $\boxed{G}$ $\boxed{C}$
F A F E G E C D C C C

Rondo from Orchestral Suite No. 2

D_2 C# B [A]C# E_2 D_2 C#

[b]D_2 F# E_2 F# G_2 [D]F# E_2 D_2 F#

E_2 D_2 E_2 F# [A]E_2 D_2 C# E_2 D_2 C# B

[A]C# E_2 D_2 C# [b]D_2 F# E_2 F# G_2

[b]F# B [F#]C# A# [b]B D C# B

[A]C# E_2 D_2 C# [b]D_2 F# E_2 F# G_2

[D]F# E_2 D_2 F# E_2 D_2 E_2 F#

[A]E_2 D_2 C# E_2 D_2 C# B [A]C# E_2 D_2 C#

[b]D_2 F# E_2 F# G_2 [b]F# B [F#]C# A#

Prelude in C Major

[C] C E G C_2 E_2 G C_2 E_2 C E G C_2 E_2

G C_2 E_2 [d] C D A_2 D_2 F_2 A D_2 F_2 C D A

D_2 F_2 A D_2 F_2 [G] B_{-2} D G D_2 F_2 G D_2 F_2

B_{-2} D G D_2 F_2 G D_2 F_2 [C] C E G C_2 E_2 G C_2

E_2 C E G C_2 E_2 G C_2 E_2 [a] C E A E_2 A_2 A

E_2 A_2 C E A E_2 A_2 A E_2 A_2 [D] C D F# A D_2

F# A D_2 C D F# A D_2 F# A D_2 [G] B_{-2} D G D_2

G_2 G D_2 G_2 B_{-2} D G D_2 G_2 G D_2 G_2 [e] B_{-2}

C E G C_2 E G C_2 B_{-2} C E G C_2 E G C_2

Waltz of the flowers

[C] E_2 B D_2 A [G] C_2 F B C_2 B A# B

[G] F_2 C_2 E_2 B [C] D_2 G C_2 D_2 C_2 B C_2

[C] E_2 B D_2 A [G] C_2 F B C_2 B A# B

[f] F_2 C_2 F_2 C# [A#] F_2 D_2 G_2 G A B C_2 D_2

[C] E_2 B D_2 A [G] C_2 F B C_2 B A# B

[G] F_2 C_2 E_2 B [C] D_2 G C_2 D_2 C_2 B C_2

[C] E_2 B D_2 A [G] C_2 F B C_2 B A# B

[a] A_2 G_2 A_2 G_2 [G] B_2 G_2 G# A_2 B_2 [C] C_3

Turkish march

B A G# A $\overset{\boxed{a}}{C}_2$ D_2 C_2 B C_2

E_2 F_2 E_2 D# E_2 $\overset{\boxed{a}}{B}_2$ A_2 G# B_2 A_2 G# A_2

C_3 A C_3 $\overset{\boxed{e}}{B}_2$ A_2 G_2 A_2

B_2 A_2 G_2 A_2 $\overset{\boxed{e}}{B}_2$ A_2 G_2 F#

E_2 B A G# A $\overset{\boxed{a}}{C}_2$ D_2 C_2 B C_2

E_2 F_2 E_2 D# E_2 $\overset{\boxed{a}}{B}_2$ A_2 G# A_2 B_2 A_2 G# A_2

C_3 A_2 C_3 $\overset{\boxed{e}}{B}_2$ A_2 G_2 A_2

B_2 A_2 G_2 A_2 $\overset{\boxed{e}}{B}_2$ A_2 G_2 F#

Place for notes:

Place for notes:

_____

_____

_____

_____

_____

_____

_____

_____

_____

_____

_____

_____

_____

Have you already played all the songs here?
See also other books with letter notes:

Christmas carols
Simple songs for children and beginners
Popular international songs

You can also try playing ordinary notes on a staff

All this can be found at: playinoneday.com

Made in the USA
Monee, IL
17 September 2023